Embracing
the
Good News

The Journey Study Series

Embracing
the
Good News

A Thomas Nelson Study Series
Based on *The Journey*
by
BILLY GRAHAM

THOMAS NELSON
Since 1798

NASHVILLE   DALLAS   MEXICO CITY   RIO DE JANEIRO   BEIJING

Published in Nashville, Tennessee. Thomas Nelson is a trademark of Thomas Nelson, Inc.

Thomas Nelson, Inc., titles may be purchased in bulk for educational, business, fund-raising, or sales promotional use. For information, please e-mail SpecialMarkets@ThomasNelson.com.

Embracing the Good News: A Thomas Nelson Study Series Based on The Journey *by Billy Graham*

ISBN-13: 978-1-4185-1773-1
ISBN-10: 1-4185-1773-9

Printed in the United States of America

07 08 09 10 11 RRD 5 4 3 2 1

Contents

1

A
New
Beginning

To GET THE MOST FROM THIS STUDY GUIDE, READ pages 53–55 of *The Journey*.

> *People come to Christ in many different ways: your experience won't necessarily be like mine. The important thing is not how we come to Christ, but that we do come, and that we are sure we are now trusting Christ for our salvation.*
>
> BILLY GRAHAM
> *The Journey*

THINK ABOUT IT

The old nature must be cast aside as a complete wreck, and good for nothing, and the man made a new creation in Christ Jesus. But willing as we may be to admit this truth, few lessons are harder to learn.

—J. GREGORY MANTLE[1]

He who was seated on the throne said, "I am making everything new!"

—REVELATION 21:5

New beginnings are a mix of emotions as excitement and fear collide. We can be excited about the opportunity to start over while being afraid to step away from comfortable surroundings. These emotions accompany any life change—new jobs, homes, schools, relationships, neighbors, family members, and so forth.

Can these emotions collide at the point of salvation? Is it possible that people sometimes see the value of their pending spiritual decision while being somewhat concerned about the changes the decision encompasses? Change is normal, yet it can be scary. Personal change can be desired yet difficult to embrace. Change is one of the most constant uncertainties a human can encounter, even if that change results in eternal life.

REWIND

Think back to your life before becoming a Christian. Place an X on the line indicating how much have you changed.

0% -- 100%

When God moves in, things can't remain the same. For some people, the change might be significant; for others, it might be less noticeable. The degree of change can vary, but the fact that something has changed can't be denied.

Some people, anxious to obtain eternal life, enter into a relationship with God without welcoming the change He brings. Doing so is like having two people in a rowboat paddling in different directions. All you do is go in circles and grow more and more frustrated. There certainly is benefit to change, but how badly do we really want it?

Journey through God's Word

One of the most used but misunderstood terms in Christianity is *hypocrisy*. It is defined as pretending to be a better person than one is in reality. The term is rooted in the Greek word meaning "to give an answer."

In the Greek culture, a hypocrite was any number of things—an interpreter of dreams, a public speaker, or an actor. Over time, the term gained a negative connotation.

In the Bible, *hypocrite* is used in the negative sense. In the Old Testament, the term can be interchanged with *ungodly*. The ungodly person either opposed or ignored God.

In the New Testament, hypocrisy as a concept is much more prevalent. Jesus addressed the hypocrisy of the pious people who held themselves in higher esteem than they should have (Matthew 6:2, 5, 16). Hypocrites were more interested in public acclaim than godly humility. Hypocrites were judgmental of others and failed to live what they claimed to believe.

Hypocrites could interpret weather but were unable to see the signs of the times (Luke 12:56). The religious leaders were criticized for not living up to the message they proclaimed (Matthew 23:3–28). Peter listed hypocrisy as an attitude that believers should avoid (1 Peter 2:1).

The opposite of hypocrisy is sincerity. Christian love, faith, and wisdom should be expressed without hypocrisy[2] (Romans 12:9; 1 Timothy 1:5; James 3:17).

Hypocrisy has been and still is counterproductive to authentic faith. We often hold others to standards that we can't live up to. We look for excuses to explain away our behaviors while being critical of those who do the same things we do. This is modern-day hypocrisy and must be avoided if we are going to positively affect our culture for Christ.

We can often suggest that other people change so that their lives can reflect their faith. Yet those of us calling for change can be the most resistant to change. Before we demand that other people start over, we must be sure we have done the same.

RETHINK

What do you expect to happen in the lives of other people when they accept Jesus Christ?

_____

_____

_____

Have these changes happened in your life? If not, why not?

_____

_____

_____

Salvation experiences vary from person to person. None is more dramatic than that of Saul of Tarsus. Saul's job was to persecute and kill Christians. He traveled from place to place making life miserable or ending the lives of those who claimed Jesus Christ as their Lord and Savior.

On the road to Damascus, Saul encountered the risen Lord face to face. Jesus asked him a question.

Read Acts 22:7. Saul was persecuting Christians, but who was taking offense?

_____

_____

_____

_____

In persecuting people, Saul was persecuting Jesus Christ. But that all changed when Saul recognized Jesus for who He was and accepted Him as Savior and Lord. For Saul, everything changed.

How has your salvation affected your . . .

Ambition?

_____

_____

_____

_____

Vocation?

_____

_____

_____

Purpose?

_____

_____

_____

Awareness of the needs of others?

_____

_____

_____

Saul got a new name, new ambition, new vocation, new purpose, and a new awareness of the real needs of other people. His

name was changed to Paul. His ambition was changed from delivering death to delivering life. His purpose went from persecuting Jesus Christ to glorifying Jesus Christ. Finally, he became aware that the greatest need in humanity was a spiritual need.

REFLECT

Authentic conversion is contagious. One of the most exciting passages in Scripture details the rapid growth of the infant church following the powerful proclamation of God's Word by Peter. This is the same Peter who had denied his relationship with Jesus when Jesus was being tried shortly before His crucifixion. What happened to Peter? He repented, accepted a change of heart, and allowed God to work through him. Let's see what happened in the early church.

As a result of Peter's preaching, the church experienced explosive growth. Acts 2:40–41 tells us that over three thousand people were added in one day! That certainly put a strain on the volunteer church staff. But they had created a plan that would train volunteers for service to God and bring them into supportive relationships with each other.

Many people who come to faith in God do not receive the kind of instruction that was provided to these early Christians. In many churches, membership requires nothing more than expressing an interest in becoming a part of the church. That wasn't enough for the early church; they embarked on a plan that would lead to the strengthening of individuals and, ultimately, the church. There were four steps in this process—four steps that we would be wise to consider in our churches today.

1. **The new believers were trained in doctrine.**
   Many people who know Jesus Christ as Lord and Savior don't know anything about their foundational beliefs. There are some issues that are central to our faith. These are the main points about which most Christians agree. Then there are secondary matters of church practice that are important but are issues of interpretation.

It was (and is) important that believers come to understand the identity of Jesus Christ. There is a huge difference in viewing Him as Savior and Lord and viewing Him as a good man or a prophet. Any faith that denies the deity of Jesus Christ denies the very truths of Scripture.

Read Acts 2:42. What are the key elements of doctrine to which you hold?

_____

_____

_____

What are the key elements to which your church holds?

_____

_____

_____

If you don't know the answers to these questions, how can you find out?

_____

_____

_____

2. **The new believers were trained in fellowship.**
   Fellowship is defined as the sharing in the lives of other believers. It is vital that believers support one another and invest time getting to know each other. Fellowship is more than a covered-dish meal in a large room of the church. When difficulties come, believers need the support system the community of faith provides. Many of the experiences you face

uniquely qualify you to minister to the needs of your fellow believers. By being in close relationships with each other, we are able to support each other in times of need.

What are some significant events that have happened in your life that have served to prepare you for ministry to other believers?

_____

_____

_____

_____

What are some things you do to invest in the lives of other believers?

_____

_____

_____

_____

How important is it for you to be in fellowship with other believers?

_____

_____

_____

_____

What is the danger of being known by other Christians? What is the benefit?

_____

_____

_____

_____

3. **The new believers were trained in the breaking of bread.**

   This most likely is a reference to the Lord's Supper as described in 1 Corinthians.

Why is the observance of the Lord's Supper important?

_____

_____

_____

_____

Read 1 Corinthians 11:23–26. What is the purpose of the Lord's Supper?

_____

_____

_____

_____

What goes through your mind when you are partaking in the Lord's Supper?

_____

_____

_____

_____

_____ This is going to take too long.

_____ This is unnecessary.

_____ This is just a ceremony.

_____ This draws my mind to the sacrifice of Jesus Christ on the cross.

4. **The new believers were trained in the discipline of prayer.**

   From the early days, corporate prayer was an integral part of the life of the Christian and the church. Prayer is communication with God. (There is a six-lesson study on prayer included in The Journey Bible Study Series.)

What was the last thing that happened that caused you to seek God in prayer?

_____

_____

_____

What is prayer? (Check all that apply.)

_____ An opportunity to tell God what I need

_____ An opportunity to tell God about my problems

_____ An opportunity to listen to God

_____ An opportunity to worship God

Prayer is one of the most misunderstood disciplines in the Christian life. That is why the apostles invested time teaching the new believers what it meant to pray. Churches that are interested in growing disciples will do likewise.

REACT

Remember: It doesn't matter how you come to Christ but that you come to Christ on His terms. We don't have the option of giving God part of our lives; it's all or nothing. Too many people go through life wondering if their commitment to Christ is real or if they are being fooled into believing they are saved when they really are not. There is no need to be confused; you can know you are saved!

Think back on your conversion experience. Who were the people who were instrumental in your conversion experience?

_____

_____

_____

_____

Who were those teachers who invested their time teaching you the simple truths of the faith?

_____

_____

_____

_____

How have you grown in your faith?

_____

_____

_____

Satan wants to convince you that your commitment to God is weak or doesn't exist. He wants to rob you of the joy of your salvation. Distraction is his main mode of operation.

When you experience doubts about your faith, you need to recall your answers to these questions. Remember the people God has used to guide you and the things that God has done on your behalf. Keep a prayer journal so that you can be reminded of God's intervention in the everyday details of life. The more aware of God you are each day, the more prepared you are to deal with the doubts you face.

Is anything different? Is God working in your life? When God moves in, you'll never be the same.

> _The Christian life is one of constant growth. If you have given your life to Christ, you are a new creation—whether you feel like it or not._
>
> BILLY GRAHAM
> _The Journey_

What are three truths you learned in this study, and how will you apply each truth to your daily life?

1. _____

_____

_____

_____

2. _____

_____

_____

_____

3. _____

_____

_____

_____

2

Is Anything Different?

T O GET THE MOST FROM THIS STUDY GUIDE, READ pages 55–56 of *The Journey*.

Perhaps you felt very close to God when you first believed in Christ, but now those feelings have faded, and you wonder if your faith was real. But listen: Certain things do happen when we give our lives to Christ, and if we understand what they are, it will give us a solid foundation against every doubt Satan hurls at us.

BILLY GRAHAM
The Journey

THINK ABOUT IT

You can't change circumstances and you can't change people, but God can change you.

—EVELYN A. THIESSEN[1]

Therefore, if anyone is in Christ, he is a new creation; the old has gone, the new has come!

—2 CORINTHIANS 5:17

We don't mind change as long as it doesn't affect us. We're not bothered by the changes people experience in order to accommodate us. We're not bothered by changes that don't involve us. But ask some people to change, and there is going to be a battle.

It is common to get several years into a faith relationship with God and to begin to wonder if anything really took place at your conversion. You don't see any evidence that anything has been renewed. You think the same way you did before your salvation. You tell the same jokes, have the same friends, do the same things. God seems to be an addendum tacked onto the latter chapters of your life. If faith in God necessitates change, why do you feel the same way you've always felt?

REWIND

On a scale of 1 to 10, with 10 being the high point, use the box below to plot your spiritual life over the past 12 months.

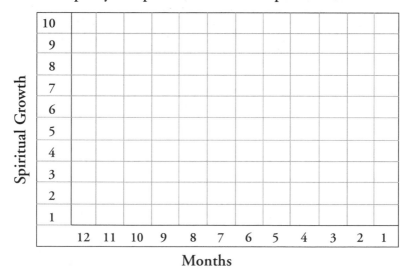

Mark the high spots and explain the events that were taking place when you were at your spiritual high points.

_____

_____

_____

_____

Mark the low spots and explain the events that were taking place when you were at your spiritual low points.

_____

_____

_____

_____

Certain things happen when you give your life to Jesus Christ. Understanding these things will help you withstand periods of doubt. Even though you don't feel like a new creation, you are one. Before you became a believer in Jesus Christ, you were destined for hell. There was nothing you could do to stop that inevitability. Now, however, you have a new destiny—heaven. If nothing else changed, that would be enough!

JOURNEY THROUGH GOD'S WORD

We don't use the term a lot, but the salvation experience can be described as *regeneration*. In regeneration, God acts to give new life to a person. God's action is the work of the Holy Spirit. Throughout the Old Testament and the New Testament, people are regenerated, or made new. Regeneration is a sudden and complete event that occurs at the moment salvation occurs. Though new birth is complete, the process of being made new by God's Spirit is a process of spiritual maturity.

The Greek word for *regeneration* in respect to individuals is only used in Titus 3:5. Though this is the only use of the Greek term, the concept is consistent with other terminology that is translated as "born again," "born of God," "renewed," and others. Jesus told Nicodemus that his entrance into God's kingdom required regeneration. The term selected by Jesus is translated as "born again" (John 3:3–8). Peter reflected the same thought in 1 Peter 1:23. The teaching throughout Scripture is consistent—to enter the kingdom of God, a person must be regenerated or made new.

In Ephesians 2:1, Paul referred to the state of being prior to regeneration as being spiritually dead and unable to interact with God. Regeneration is passive on the part of the human. Only God can initiate the act of spiritual renewal.

The psalmist requested that God create in him a new heart. This is a request for regeneration (Psalm 51:10).

Only after regeneration can a person have a friendly relationship with the Creator. Regeneration is not the end, but rather the beginning of an eternal relationship with God the Father. There is no other way to enter into a relationship with God but through regeneration.[2]

A change in your eternal destination is nothing to take lightly. We can live day to day with confidence because of our relationship with God and the peace He brings into our lives. But what should you do when you begin to wonder if your commitment is authentic? That's what this lesson is all about.

RETHINK

Have you ever doubted your faith or questioned the stability of your relationship with Him? If so, what caused you to question your faith?

_____

_____

_____

If someone told you he or she was questioning their faith, how would you guide them to resolve their questions?

_____

_____

_____

Even people with dynamic, thriving faith can question their faith relationship with God. Sometimes God seems distant or uncaring, prayers go unanswered, and problems arise. Life captures our attention, and our relationship with God becomes secondary. It's not an intentional drift, but a subtle shift in one's attention to God.

Evaluate your life right now. What issues are demanding your attention?

_____

_____

_____

_____

How are these issues affecting your relationship with God?

_____

_____

_____

_____

REFLECT

Sometimes we need to be reminded of all the things God did when He moved into our lives. God isn't satisfied to be given a closet or a small compartment of our lives; He moves into all of it, or He doesn't move in at all.

This creates some problems for many people because they want to maintain control of certain areas of life. Maybe a person has a well-paying, high-profile job and fears God will call him or her to a ministry position where the reward isn't monetary. Some people fear God will redirect them to a new community, state, or nation. Some people want all God has to offer without having to change anything about themselves. These attitudes serve to quench the Holy Spirit in our lives and create distance between us and God. Disobedience and not listening to God are sins, and sin separates us from God. Let's consider a few changes that salvation brings.

1. **A change of heart**

   We talked in an earlier lesson about the heart and the change that takes place when we allow the Holy Spirit to enter into our lives.

Read Ezekiel 36:26 and describe the change that is described in this verse.

_____

_____

_____

A heart of stone is a heart hardened to God and His purposes for us. Until you have a "heart transplant," you cannot have godly compassion on the hurting or godly love for the needy. This change of heart is easily resisted and, when resisted, puts out the fire that the Holy Spirit is stoking in our souls.

In what ways is your heart changed? If it is no different, what should you do to restore the fire that God wants to burn in your soul?

_____

_____

_____

_____

_____

2. **A change of vision**

   Before we enter into a relationship with God, our vision is limited. But once the Holy Spirit moves in, things change.

Read John 3:3. What aspect of a person's vision changes when he or she experiences salvation?

_____

_____

_____

Seeing the kingdom of God is the same as perceiving spiritual things. The fact is that salvation is required if a person is going to be able to see spiritual things. We all know what it's like to enter into a conversation with someone who cannot understand spiritual matters. No matter how hard you try to explain it, there is no way to make him or her understand. This is why unbelievers can't understand God's Word—they lack the capacity to understand spiritual things.

One way to check our spiritual growth is by evaluating our understanding of spiritual things. If the Holy Spirit is alive within you, spiritual things will be easier to understand. However, there are some mysteries of God that people will never understand—saved or not.

3. **A change of purpose**

We enter into this life demanding our way. Babies cry to call their parents' attention to their needs. No one has to teach us to be self-centered; it comes naturally. As we mature, the attention to self seldom diminishes. For some people, they are just as focused on themselves as adults as they were when they were babies. They cry, whine, demand their way, and expect the world to conform to them.

Reread 2 Corinthians 5:17. How does salvation affect one's purpose?

_____

_____

_____

Before salvation, our purpose in life was to please ourselves. After salvation, the Holy Spirit works in us to redirect our attention from pleasing ourselves to pleasing God. Notice that Paul doesn't say that we have been overhauled; he says we have been made new.

There are some situations in life that demand a complete redo. People sometimes choose to demolish a home and rebuild it rather than renovate it. God doesn't attempt to renovate us because there is nothing in us that warrants repair. Instead, God chooses to start over and make us a new creation—that's better than renovation.

The problem for many believers is that they try to salvage certain aspects of their past lives. They want the experience of salvation, the indwelling of the Holy Spirit, but they want to keep their old ways of life.

To what are you clinging from your life before salvation?

_____

_____

_____

_____

_____ Relationships

_____ Habits

_____ Social life

_____ Vocabulary

_____ Entertainment

_____ Employment

_____ Personality traits

_____ Other: _____

REACT

Is anything different in your life? Maybe working through this lesson has helped you see that there are some things you are doing to prevent the Holy Spirit from working in your life. Maybe you are being resistant to the changes He wants to bring about in you.

Why would you resist the changes associated with faith in God?

_____ It scares me to think about giving up what I have.

_____ It scares me to think about starting over with new relationships and values.

_____ I can't get free from my addictions, habits, or preferences.

_____ All I want is eternal life when I die; I'm not interested in changing anything now.

_____ Other: _____

If you are resisting the Holy Spirit, you cannot grow in your faith. You can't move forward while looking back. What is in front of you is so much more than you ever imagined. God has your best life laid out in front of you; anything you are clinging to is so much less than what God has. Because He loves you, He wants the best for you. Life might still have its share of problems, but there is no life like the one totally committed to God.

Change isn't an option; it is required. When God moves in, everything changes. Therefore, if nothing has changed, it could be that God never moved in. Don't go through life thinking that you have taken care of this matter; be sure about it. Ask God to help you be certain about your relationship with Him. Call on a pastor or spiritual mentor to help talk through the situation. It's too important to leave unsettled.

After salvation, the Holy Spirit works in us to redirect our attention from pleasing ourselves to pleasing God.
BILLY GRAHAM
The Journey

What are three truths you learned in this study, and how will you apply each truth to your daily life?

1. _____

_____

_____

_____

2. _____

_____

_____

_____

3. _____

_____

_____

_____

3

A
New
Relationship

To GET THE MOST FROM THIS STUDY GUIDE, READ pages 56–58 of *The Journey*.

> *The first thing that happens when we give our lives to Christ is that God gives us a new relationship. Instead of being God's enemy, you are now His friend, and He is now yours.*
>
> BILLY GRAHAM
> *The Journey*

THINK ABOUT IT

In a world that is focused on improved techniques and newer and newer technologies, there has never been discovered a shortcut to building relationships—not with people, and especially not with God.

—JOE HESH[1]

Remember that at that time you were separate from Christ, excluded from citizenship in Israel and foreigners to the covenants of the promise, without hope and without God in the world.

—EPHESIANS 2:12

If you've ever traveled to a different country, you know what it is like to be a stranger because of language, customs, or traditions. As the strangers, it is our responsibility to adapt to the situation, not the other way around. We must be willing to learn the language, accept the customs, and honor the traditions of the land we are visiting.

From God's perspective, every person who is not born again is a stranger. There are only two ways this problem might be corrected—either the person changes or God changes. It's easy to see which one is required! In order to no longer be aliens to God, we must be willing to accept His offer of salvation on His terms. There are no negotiations—it's God's way or no way. And He has opened the way to us because He loves us.

REWIND

What are the primary characteristics of a good relationship?

_____

_____

_____

What are the primary characteristics of a good relationship with God?

_____

_____

_____

Which is easier to establish and maintain—a good relationship with a person or a good relationship with God?

_____

_____

_____

Relationships are always in the news for one of several reasons— a new relationship between high-profile people begins or ends, there is public trouble within a relationship, a service wants to help you find the person for the perfect relationship . . . the list goes on and on.

One of the best things about becoming a believer in Jesus Christ is the effect He has on our relationships. Not only do we get a new relationship with Him, but we have a new perspective on relationships with other people. The real key to relationship success is God's involvement in every aspect of the relationship. Otherwise, our relationships are fighting a losing battle.

JOURNEY THROUGH GOD'S WORD

In the Bible, an *alien* is a person who is living in a culture that is not his own. The term also can be translated as *foreigner* or *stranger*. Several biblical characters are identified as aliens:

1. When Elijah was in the home of the widow, he was an alien (1 Kings 17:20).

2. Isaac was an alien to the Philistine king, Abimelech (Genesis 26:3).

3. Abraham, Isaac, and Jacob were aliens in the Promised Land (Genesis 20:1).

Israel began as aliens in Egypt and, after making the journey to Canaan, was generally welcoming to aliens as long as the special rules for dealing with aliens were observed (Deuteronomy 24:19–20). Aliens were entitled to hearings in the judicial system and were expected to abide by the laws of the host land.

Every person is or has been an alien to God. We see in the Old Testament that aliens were expected to abide by the Sabbath laws and worship regulations. They could observe celebrations such as Passover and were required to abide by societal laws.

In the New Testament, believers are referred to as aliens and temporary residents of Earth. What does this mean? It means believers must live by the rules of the host—the nation in which we live—without compromising their faith in God. It means that believers are not to get attached to the physical aspects of Earth because it is not their home. Believers are to be model citizens while longing for the day when they can go to their ultimate home—heaven with God.[2]

The problem many believers have is that they are too connected to the world in which they live. They invest their lives storing up possessions and prestige rather than making a difference for God. This is the recipe for spiritual frustration and leads many believers to question their relationships with God.

We spend a lot of time trying to get people to conform to our expectations in relationships. We even do that with God. We expect Him to mold Himself into the image we have created.

We want a relationship that is regulated by us—and that just doesn't sit very well with God.

RETHINK

Describe your relationship with God.

_____

_____

_____

What are the major strengths in your relationship with Him?

_____

_____

_____

What are the major weaknesses in your relationship with Him?

_____

_____

_____

Most people enjoy the company of a good friend. Friends are those people with whom we share our lives—the good and the bad. It is interesting, then, that the Bible describes us as being God's friends.

What do you share with human friends that you don't share with God?

_____

_____

_____

Consider your friendship with God. Which term best describes your relationship?

_____ Strangers

_____ Acquaintances

_____ Co-workers

_____ Best friends

Because of what Jesus Christ did for us, we can be friends with God. That is something that should bring joy to us every day.

REFLECT

James 2:23 tells us that Abraham was considered a friend of God. What does it mean to be God's friend? In John 15:11–17, Jesus expands on what it means to be His friend.

Friendship with God is the source of real joy (John 15:11). Jesus wanted His disciples to be full of joy. Serving God should never be drudgery. How many times, however, have we been more focused on complaining than on being obedient?

What are things you do that bring you joy?

_____

_____

_____

Is obeying God on your list? Why or why not?

_____

_____

_____

We search for joy in all kinds of places and situations. Some people realize that a relationship can bring them joy, but they never consider a relationship with God. You might be one of those people who can't seem to discover real joy in your life. The key is investing your life in things that matter to God rather than things that matter to you or other people. When you finally turn your life over to God, you will discover that real joy can exist in your life.

Friendship with God requires love (John 15:12). The Bible doesn't suggest that we love each other; it demands it! If we aren't loving others, we are being disobedient to God's command. Disobedience is sin, and sin separates us from God. You can't be God's friend and not love other people.

In what situations is it most difficult for you to love someone?

_____

_____

_____

_____

_____

How can you cultivate an attitude of love toward people who are difficult to love?

_____

_____

_____

_____

Jesus had every reason not to love people. People were the primary sources of problems in His ministry. The disciples doubted, the Jews persecuted, the government officials ridiculed Him . . . why should Jesus love these people? Why should He love us?

He has no choice but to love us because love is part of God's character. If Jesus doesn't love us, He isn't fully God!

Friendship with God requires obedience (John 15:14). Jesus offered a condition of friendship—obedience. He said, "You are my friends if . . ." We live in a time when we enter into contractual agreements that are regulated by confusing terms and conditions. We agree to the conditions because we want the service or the item. But what about friendships? Do they come with terms and conditions?

What are the conditions of your friendships with other people?

_____

_____

_____

_____

What are the conditions you have to meet in order to be friends with certain people?

_____

_____

_____

_____

Friendship with Jesus requires obedience. Jesus said it this way . . . "If you obey Me, you are My friends."

Fill in the blank: The above statement can be restated as "If

you disobey me, _____ .

> *If we have given our lives to Christ, God has adopted us into His family. At one time we were (so to speak) spiritual orphans. We weren't part of God's family, and we had no right to expect anything from Him. But He is now your loving heavenly Father, and you are now His child, spiritually reborn into His family.*
>
> Billy Graham
> *The Journey*

In addition to being God's friends, we are His children. We are both born and adopted. We are reborn spiritually (1 Peter 1:23) then adopted into God's family (Ephesians 1:5). Adoption is necessary because we have no natural connection to God and we are initially His enemies. However, because of His Son, Jesus Christ, we are welcomed into the family as adopted children. This new relationship with God empowers us to live with a new sense of purpose.

Read Ephesians 5:1. What is the universal purpose of all believers?

_____ To follow their desires

_____ To be imitators of God

_____ To visit God weekly

_____ To call on God when necessary

Because we are God's friends, we gain a second benefit of salvation—new citizenship in the kingdom of God.

What are the privileges and responsibilities associated with citizenship?

_____

_____

_____

_____

In the early church, Roman citizenship was prized because citizens of Rome paid fewer taxes and automatically became officers in the Roman army. A Roman citizen couldn't be flogged or crucified. If found guilty in a trial, a Roman citizen could immediately appeal to Caesar. Paul did this on one occasion because he was a Roman citizen (Acts 25:11). Jesus wanted His followers to value kingdom citizenship above Roman citizenship.

Read Mark 1:15 and Philippians 3:20. Since our citizenship is in heaven, how should we live on Earth?

_____

_____

_____

Read Acts 5:29. How should we respond when there is a conflict between biblical values and human instruction?

_____ Obey the human instruction

_____ Obey the biblical value

_____ Search for a compromise

_____ Do nothing

A new relationship and a new citizenship are two of the things we receive when we enter into a faith relationship with God. We can live with joy in difficult times because of the fact that God is closer than we ever imagined He would be. In the trials and in the good times, God is there wanting for us the best He has to offer. That's how much He loves us.

REACT

In many churches, there are people who seem bored. They don't worship, don't participate, don't celebrate God's presence, don't interact with other people. Their approach to worship is a lot like keeping a good-luck charm—it's done to keep something bad from happening.

It seems absurd that people would reduce their relationships with God to a game of chance, but it happens every day in churches like yours and mine. Obviously, these people have missed out on what it means to be God's friend.

In the space below, write a friendship note to God expressing how you feel about Him.

_____

_____

_____

_____

_____

God's desire is for you to be His best friend. He wants to be the first place you turn when the bottom drops out and the first place you turn to celebrate life's victories. He wants to be your first thought in the morning, your last thought at night, and your conscience throughout the day. All He asks is that you submit to His rule in your life. Is the benefit worth the trade? Absolutely!

It begins with your acknowledgment of your need for God in your life. It continues as you ask Him to forgive you of your sin and to come into your life. It is lived out as you rely on Him each day for everything you need. It's the model of spiritual maturity that will strengthen us to handle every aspect of life.

As long as we are on this earth, we possess dual citizenship. On one hand we owe allegiance to our nation and are called to be good citizens. But we are also citizens of the kingdom of God, that invisible kingdom of which Christ is the head. Our supreme loyalty is to Him.

BILLY GRAHAM
The Journey

What are three truths you learned in this study, and how will you apply each truth to your daily life?

1. _____

_____

_____

_____

2. _____

_____

_____

_____

3. _____

_____

_____

_____

4

A
New
Family

To GET THE MOST FROM THIS STUDY GUIDE, READ pages 58–59 of *The Journey*.

You are never alone if you know Christ. You are part of God's family, with brothers and sisters in Christ who love you and want to help you, if you will let them.

BILLY GRAHAM
The Journey

THINK ABOUT IT

One of the reasons our society has become such a mess is that we're isolated from each other.

—MAGGIE KUHN[1]

Consequently, you are no longer foreigners and aliens, but fellow citizens with God's people and members of God's household.

—EPHESIANS 2:19

As children, we all probably entertained the idea of trading in our families for new ones. We might not have wanted to trade family member for family member. Maybe you offered your sister in exchange for a baseball card or your brother in exchange for a doll. We laugh at this concept, but it actually crosses the mind of almost everyone at some point.

A new family, however, isn't too far out of reach. It's not a trade; it's an addition. When you become a Christian, you inherit a universal family of people who share the same relationship with God through Jesus Christ. It doesn't matter what color your skin is or where you live—we are all a part of the same family.

There is a difference between being a member of the family of God and being a church member. You can be a church member without being a member of the family of God. That's a question each individual must address. However, Scripture clearly teaches that authentic faith in God leads to a desire to be in fellowship with fellow believers. Therefore, claiming to be a member of the family of God without having the desire to be a part of a local congregation is a contradiction, and it will stunt our spiritual growth.

REWIND

Being a member of God's family provides you with a multitude of brothers and sisters. What does this mean to you?

_____

_____

_____

Few people embrace the idea of being alone in life. Everyone wants someone who cares about them and can be an encouragement to them. We look for companionship with people like us. As believers, we share the most important of all characteristics—a family heritage that links us to God. This is the fellowship of the saints.

JOURNEY THROUGH GOD'S WORD

Christians are bound together in the fellowship of faith. Fellowship is related to the Hebrew concept of sharing a house in which the study of God's Word took place. In the New Testament, the term for _fellowship_ was most often used by Paul to describe the relationship between believers

---

and Jesus Christ. Believers have fellowship with Jesus Christ (1 Corinthians 1:9), fellowship in the gospel (1 Corinthians 9:23), and fellowship with the Holy Spirit (2 Corinthians 13:14).

Paul used the word *fellowship* to describe how believers should help each other. This assistance was not limited to financial help; it included sharing with each other the truth of the gospel of Jesus Christ (Galatians 6:6).

When Paul was dependent upon the generosity of believers for his livelihood, he used the word *fellowship* to characterize their donations (Romans 15:26). The most familiar usage of the term *fellowship* is its use in describing the unity and closeness that exists between believers in Jesus Christ. Paul didn't want anything to disrupt the fellowship of the church. John supported Paul's call for fellowship and suggested that a broken fellowship is a mark of a spiritual problem in the life of a believer (1 John 3, 6–7).[2]

In the early church, unity was an issue. Some things never change. Today's church often is beset with problems because people fail to protect the fellowship of the faith. Each of us must focus more on protecting the fellowship rather than demanding our way. There is no room in the church for self-gratification and selfishness—both are contrary to the character of God.

In any family, there will be problems. The same thing happens in our spiritual families. We can get into conflict with other believers and negatively affect the fellowship of the church. Mature believers must be willing to do whatever is necessary to keep the fellowship intact.

RETHINK

What are the characteristics of a perfect family?

_____

_____

_____

Would you be in the perfect family? Why or why not?

_____

_____

_____

There is a perfect family in which you are an important part— the family of God. It is perfect not because we are perfect, but because God is perfect and His Son's sacrifice covers all our sins.

We call this family "the church." But it might not be the same church that comes to mind when you first hear the term.

In the Bible, the word *church* refers to . . .

_____ A building ("I drove by the church.")

_____ An event, such as worship ("We're going to church.")

_____ A denomination ("The church defines . . .")

_____ The entire universal family of God ("We all are part of the same church.")

It's hard to change our way of thinking about church, but we must keep in mind that the universal family of God shares the same basic beliefs in Jesus Christ and the Word of God. No singular congregation or denomination has the corner on the market . . . we're all in this together.

What are the basic beliefs held by your church and/or denomination?

_____

_____

_____

How do the beliefs above compare to the basic beliefs of a neighboring church?

_____ They are the same.

___ I don't know what the other church believes.

_____ I don't know what my church/denomination believes.

_____ There are some differences, but I'm not sure what they are.

REFLECT

The family of God is a new concept to many people. Some people get excited about the idea of sharing their faith journey with other people. Others prefer to go it alone. The reality is that our spiritual family is here for a reason. Let's look at some significant facts about the family of God.

1. **We realize the benefits of the family of God as we act in obedience to God.**
   There are benefits associated with being a part of God's family, but those benefits can't be realized if we are disobedient to God. Being a member of the family of God necessitates obedience to God's ways.

Read Matthew 12:48–50. What, if anything, surprises you about Jesus' statement regarding His disciples?

_____

_____

_____

_____

_____

Jesus was part of a family—a mother, earthly father, and brothers—yet He identified His followers as His family. This indicates that spiritual ties are stronger then genetic ties. When faced with the dilemma of being obedient to God or doing what our families want, we often choose the family. In doing so, we make the family tie stronger than the spiritual tie.

The Bible clearly teaches that a dynamic, growing faith requires making obedience to God our top priority. This is a basic concept played out throughout the Bible. There were some people who, when faced with the choice between God and family, chose God. Some chose family, possessions, or self-gratification—all acts of disobedience to God.

When given the choice between your family members and your faith, how would you respond? Explain your reasoning.

_____

_____

_____

_____

_____

We can't be disobedient to God and enjoy the benefits of a relationship with Him. When we choose anything over our allegiance to God, we make a choice to live with the consequences of our sin. Sin's consequences are immediate and permanent. Immediately, we are distanced from God; permanently, we often are scarred with the tangible consequences of our sin.

Like the chorus of a song, the idea of obedience to God keeps coming back around. It is obviously one of the most important concepts in Scripture.

2. **As members of the family of God, we are heirs with Jesus Christ.**

   An heir is entitled to all that the father has. The same is true in the spiritual sense. When we accept Jesus

Christ as Lord and Savior, we become fellow heirs
with Him. This fact escapes many people because
God provides so much more than worldly security—
He provides peace, purpose, guidance, forgiveness,
love, and more. He also meets our daily needs, provides for our unexpected needs, and communicates
with us on a regular basis.

What do you expect to inherit from God?

_____

_____

_____

_____

What are you passing along to others from God?

_____

_____

_____

_____

Read Romans 8:15–17. What is the ultimate benefit of being an heir of God?

_____

_____

_____

_____

The main difference between being an heir of God and being the heir of a person is that as God's heirs we don't have to wait to receive the inheritance. Once we accept Jesus Christ as Lord and Savior, we receive access to God's blessings and assurance of spending eternity in heaven with Him. God's blessings are the way that He works through us to affect the world around us. As we are blessed, we reveal Him to others, and that is our ultimate purpose.

3. **When we become members of the family of God, all barriers are broken down.**

   We have many criteria by which we separate people. Some lines are drawn along socioeconomic status. Other lines are motivated by race or national origin. Some people draw lines based on someone's gender. Lines have existed between schools, states, nations, and political parties. Just about the time a barrier is broken down, a new one is erected in its place. Yet, God never intended for there to be barriers. Not only does God desire no barriers be between people, He also desires no barrier be between Him and us. Because God loves all people, it is impossible to erect barriers and be obedient to God.

Read Ephesians 2:19–22. What does the family of God include?

_____

_____

_____

What is your role in this family?

_____ I'm in charge.

_____ I'm the bratty child.

_____ I'm the whiny baby.

_____ I'm a full member of the family.

It is easy to forget that we all are a part of the same family, because we tend to organize ourselves in ways that separate us from other believers. You probably have seen a picture of a street with different churches on each corner. Believe it or not, the differences that separate congregation from congregation are usually minimal—matters of church practice, not theology. Rather than look for what separates us, we should look for those points on which we agree and celebrate being members of God's family.

REACT

> In my travels I have often met men and women who were very different from me. And yet after a few minutes it was almost as if we had known each other all our lives. Why? Because we both knew Christ. Our common spiritual bond cut through the barriers that separated us, and we enjoyed fellowship as members of God's family.
>
> BILLY GRAHAM
> *The Journey*

As believers in God, we have a universal support structure that is unified in its desire to please and serve God. Christianity is not a competition between individuals, congregations, or denominations. When we lose site of our purpose and focus on these issues, we are being distracted from our ultimate purpose.

How much of each day of your life is invested in maintaining your relationship with the family of God?

0% ------- 25% ------- 50% ------- 75% ------- 100%

How much of each day of your life is invested in things that matter only to you?

0% ------- 25% ------- 50% ------- 75% ------- 100%

What is revealed by your responses to the questions above?

_____

_____

_____

Many individuals, congregations, and denominations have lost sight of what really matters and instead focus their energies on issues rather than reaching out to a hurting world. Some Christian businesses are more focused on the business than the ministry. No wonder so many people in today's world are skeptical about Christianity.

Spiritual change begins with individuals, and the only individual I can change is me; the only individual you can change is you. We must work on strengthening our relationships with our heavenly Father in order to make a significant difference in the world around us.

Everyone who truly believes in Jesus Christ is your spiritual brother or sister. We are bound together in God's family, not by an organization, but by a spiritual relationship.

BILLY GRAHAM
The Journey

What are three truths you learned in this study, and how will you apply each truth to your daily life?

1. _____

_____

_____

_____

_____

2. _____

_____

_____

_____

3. _____

_____

_____

_____

5

A
New
Purpose

T O GET THE MOST FROM THIS STUDY GUIDE, READ
pages 59–61 of *The Journey*.

Some people are very focused, using all their energies to reach their goals. Others drift through life with little purpose or direction, living for the moment and never thinking about where they are headed. Most people probably live somewhere in between. But they all have this in common: They are living only for themselves and their own happiness. But when we come to Christ, God gives us a new purpose.

BILLY GRAHAM
The Journey

THINK ABOUT IT

Have a purpose in life, and having it, throw into your work such strength of mind and muscle as God has given you.

—THOMAS CARLYLE[1]

*For we are God's workmanship, created in Christ Jesus to
do good works, which God prepared in advance for us to do.*
—EPHESIANS 2:10

Everyone is searching for purpose. Within the business world, consultants are busy helping develop purpose or mission statements that guide the work of the business. Career coaches advise people to develop a personal purpose or mission statement. Churches, schools, and social organizations all are looking for ways to identify their purposes so that their activities can be governed.

Do you know your purpose in life? It isn't a trick question. Before you became a Christian, your purpose in life was self-centered. You lived to take care of your own needs and to make your own decisions. However, your purpose in life was redefined the moment you accepted Jesus Christ as your Lord and Savior. His purpose is now your purpose. How you carry out that purpose is a matter of your vocational choice.

REWIND

What is *your* purpose in life in regard to . . .

1. Family?

_____

_____

_____

2. Finances?

_____

_____

_____

3. Faith?

_____

_____

_____

4. Future?

_____

_____

_____

What is *God's* purpose for your life in regard to . . .

1. Family?

_____

_____

_____

2. Finances?

_____

_____

_____

3. Faith?

_____

_____

_____

4. Future?

_____

_____

_____

Explain any variations in your responses above.

_____

_____

_____

There is a difference between giving God total control of your life and adding God to your life. The first is a picture of Lordship; the second is a picture of empty religion. Empty religion has been around a long time. Both the Old Testament and the New Testament show examples of people who were more concerned about their religion than their relationship with God. The Bible never teaches us to be "religious," but to be focused on Jesus Christ.

Jesus painted a picture of a relationship with God. Through one's relationship with God, real peace and purpose are discovered. If you have a real relationship with God, you will pursue

His purposes for you; if you are practicing empty religion, your faith is self-centered. You have become a modern-day Pharisee.

JOURNEY THROUGH GOD'S WORD

Numbering nearly six thousand, the Pharisees were the largest Jewish party in New Testament times. In the Gospels, they are often viewed as the opposition to the ministry of Jesus. The apostle Paul was a member of the Pharisees (Philippians 3:5). The Pharisees primarily controlled the synagogues, but their influence was felt throughout the Jewish culture.

The first-century historian, Josephus, referred to the Pharisees, Sadducees, and Essenes as having come into existence around 150 BC. The name means "separated ones" in reference to their practice of separating themselves for the study of Scripture.

The Pharisees are credited with the transformation of Jewish religion from sacrifice-centered to law-centered. They utilized oral traditions and the written word to teach their tenets. For the Pharisees, the way to God was through obedience to the law. Though viewed today as rigid and traditional, the Pharisees were considered progressive in the first century. They were more likely to embrace change than were some of the other parties within the Jewish culture.

The Pharisees accepted the Old Testament as authentic and authoritative. They believed in one God and in life after death.

Though the Pharisees were Jews, there are modern-day Pharisees within the family of God. What makes one a modern-day Pharisee? First, a focus on legalism. Some people in today's church are very legalistic in their approaches, and Christianity gets reduced to a series of rules. Rules are important, but making our faith legalistic puts up a barrier that potential believers can't overcome, and misses the truth of God's grace. Second, a Pharisee views his or her interpretation of Scripture as the only possible interpretation. Notice this is in reference to interpretation—something that is applied to Scripture when the precise meaning may be unclear. Interpretation is important, but no one person or group can claim a degree of insight to the exclusion of anyone else.

As believers, it is important that we hold to truth as presented in God's Word, and not add to it or reduce it to a series of rules.

In today's world, we are challenged to make our faith real and relevant. Rather than building walls that keep people out, we need to make sure we throw open the doors to faith in Jesus Christ—that is humanity's greatest need.

RETHINK

What are your spiritual goals for . . .

Today?

_____

_____

_____

_____

This week?

_____

_____

_____

_____

This year?

_____

_____

_____

_____

The next five years?

_____

_____

_____

What are the things you are doing to reach those goals?

_____

_____

_____

When you accept Jesus Christ as your Lord and Savior, your purpose in life is redefined. Like we said earlier, your new purpose is the same as God's purpose because His Holy Spirit moves into your life.

Some people compartmentalize their faith and hold to their own self-directed goals. They are more than happy to participate in spiritual events when they have the time, but they are governed by their personal goals. Other people seem to have no goals in their personal or spiritual lives. They wander through life simply reacting to the events that transpire.

When it comes to your goals in life, how motivated are you?

Passive --- Focused

Maybe you thought, *Which goals?* Well, by the end of this lesson, that question should disappear. As a believer, you only have one kind of goal—God's goals for you. All the goals you now have—personal goals, financial goals, professional goals—are subsets under God's goals for you. This should make life easier to handle.

REFLECT

When we come to Christ, God gives us a new purpose. Instead of living to please ourselves, we now have the desire to please God. God begins to change our perspective on everything in life; we see people and situations differently. We don't look at life expecting to get something; we look at life with the hope that we can give.

Read Ephesians 2:10. Based on this verse, what is your purpose in life?

_____

_____

_____

_____

Read 2 Corinthians 5:14–16. What does it mean to be compelled by the love of Christ?

_____

_____

_____

_____

For whom are we told to live?

_____

_____

_____

How should our perception of other people be affected by our salvation?

_____

_____

_____

When we consider our new purpose, we can begin to wonder if we really have the power to live it out. The bad news is that we don't have the power; the good news is that God provides the power!

Becoming a Christian makes available all of the power we need to accomplish the tasks God has for us to do. We don't need an outside source in order to do what He tells us to do. As we depend on His Spirit, we will begin to see God do things through us that we never imagined possible.

The Holy Spirit is given to enable us to do God's will for our lives. We don't have to depend on our own abilities or trust our own efforts. There are several things the Holy Spirit does in regard to our lives. Let's take a look at a few of them.

The Holy Spirit helps us discern truth. There is only one truth, but it isn't always easy to find it. One of the things the Holy Spirit does to help guide us in life is showing us what the truth is.

Read John 16:13. The Holy Spirit speaks truth. That's half of the equation. What else is necessary in order for truth to penetrate your heart and mind?

_____

_____

_____

Without understanding truth, discerning your purpose in life will be impossible. Satan wants you to do anything except God's will for your life. Therefore, wrong choices can be disguised as right choices. Because they are confused, many Christians live below God's plan for their lives. They assume God wants them to keep doing the things they have always done while God has something else He wants them to do. There is a tension that comes forth in spiritual frustration.

When it comes to discerning truth, what steps do you take?

_____

_____

_____

_____

How do you know what truth really is?

_____

_____

_____

_____

The Holy Spirit guides our steps. This might seem supernatural. That's because it is supernatural! There have been times in the lives of many believers when God has ordered their steps. He has redirected people toward ministry opportunities they never saw.

Think about the direction in which you are headed in life. What role is the Holy Spirit playing in your decisions?

_____ None

_____ I seek the guidance of the Holy Spirit when things have gone all wrong.

_____ I seek the guidance of the Holy Spirit when nothing else works.

_____ I seek the guidance of the Holy Spirit before making a move.

When Peter wondered what God would have him do, God stepped in and guided his steps.

Read Acts 10:17–23. In Peter's life, we see an example of what it means to follow God. Reread the passage and identify the steps Peter took to discern God's will.

_____

_____

_____

Peter first was seeking God's direction. The story says that Peter wondered to himself. Peter didn't grow complacent in his tasks; he kept his eyes roaming and he asked, "What's next?" Second, Peter was in tune with God's Spirit. When the Holy Spirit spoke to Peter, he didn't have to seek help from someone else. Peter knew God was speaking to him because he had an intimate relationship with God. Third, Peter was obedient to what the Spirit told him to do. Peter didn't look for excuses or hesitate; he simply obeyed because he knew that anything short of immediate obedience was disobedience.

Delayed obedience is disobedience. What is the result of being disobedient to God?

_____

_____

_____

The Holy Spirit tells us where to serve. Once we know what God wants us to do, we often wonder where He wants us to serve. The Holy Spirit works to guide believers into the specific places we are to serve.

Read Acts 16:6–10. Paul attempted to carry out his ministry in places that made sense to him, but God prevented it from hap-

pening. Then Paul was called to Macedonia. Explain a time when you have had a similar experience.

_____

_____

_____

In order for Paul to hear God's direction, he had to be willing to wait. The Bible says that Paul went to Troas. This was the only choice he had. It was there that he heard from God. Again, once the call was clear, we see God's servant move immediately.

What keeps you from immediately doing what God wants you to do?

_____

_____

_____

REACT

Once we understand that our purpose in life is intricately connected to God's purposes for the world, we can rest assured that life will never be the same. God has a plan that includes using you and me to accomplish His purposes on Earth. That should be great news for anyone who knows Jesus Christ as Lord and Savior.

In the space provided, write a prayer asking God to reveal to you His plan for your life and to give you the power to do what He asks you to do.

_____

_____

_____

_____

_____

There is nothing greater than living out the purposes for which God designed you. Life is fulfilling because you know that you are making a contribution to the expansion of God's kingdom. There is real peace and contentment that comes from living out our purposes. If you aren't content in life, it might be that you aren't doing what God intended you to do with your life.

How content are you?

_____ Not at all

_____ Slightly

_____ Average

_____ Totally

Do you know for certain that you are living out God's purposes for your life? If yes, how do you know? If no, why don't you know?

_____

_____

_____

_____

> *The Spirit has been given for many reasons—but one is to help us live the way we should. We aren't meant to live the Christian life in our own strength. God has provided His Spirit to help us.*
>
> BILLY GRAHAM
> *The Journey*

What are three truths you learned in this study, and how will
you apply each truth to your daily life?

1. _____

_____

_____

_____

2. _____

_____

_____

_____

3. _____

_____

_____

_____

6

A
New
Destiny

T O GET THE MOST FROM THIS STUDY GUIDE, READ pages 61–62 of *The Journey*.

> *The word "conversion" means "change"—and the most radical change of all when we come to Christ is that God gives us a new destiny. Once we were bound for eternal separation from God; now we will live with Him forever. Once we had no hope of eternal life; now we do.*
>
> BILLY GRAHAM
> *The Journey*

THINK ABOUT IT

Destiny is not a matter of chance, it is a matter of choice; it is not a thing to be waited for, it is a thing to be achieved.
—WILLIAM JENNINGS BRYAN[1]

Therefore, there is now no condemnation for those who are in Christ Jesus.

—ROMANS 8:1

Of all the things that change when we become a Christian, the most significant is the change of destiny. It's not a subtle shift; it is radical. Whereas we previously were destined for eternity in hell separated from God, we now are destined for eternity in heaven with God.

Have you ever been headed one place, then changed your mind and gone somewhere different? Those sudden changes are so common that we often don't even think about what we're doing. The spiritual change of direction that accompanies salvation is something worthy of celebration—a daily celebration that comes forth in life.

REWIND

Eternal life is . . .

_____ **Something one must earn.**

_____ **Not available to people like me.**

_____ **A gift from God that will never be taken away.**

_____ **A nice thought, but not real.**

If getting into heaven requires our being good enough, we're all in big trouble. God is perfect and, therefore, cannot exist where there is imperfection. The very idea that we are imperfect people is enough to keep us out of heaven. We can't even count on outperforming others because God doesn't grade on the curve. The standard is perfection; there is no other option.

It's a sobering thought to realize that admission to heaven requires perfection and that perfection is impossible. We cannot go through one moment of one day without falling short of perfection's standard. Humanity is left in a hopeless state—or is it?

JOURNEY THROUGH GOD'S WORD

Eternal life is the ultimate good life. It is life the way it was intended to be lived in fellowship with God. The New Testament makes the reality of eternal life a central theme. In the books of Matthew, Mark, Luke, and John, the way in which someone obtains eternal life is redefined. Legalism is set aside in favor of grace.

The real significance of eternal life is not its duration, but its quality. Every person will experience eternity; it's the quality of that existence that must be determined. Will a person choose the best possible existence—heaven—or the worst existence—hell? It is a matter of choice.

Eternal life is both a present and future experience. Jesus said that eternal life is "knowing God" (John 17:3). The present reality is that knowing God and living in that close relationship with Him offers us a glimpse of what heaven will be like. We get to know God through experience—spending time with Him. The knowledge of God is not captured in intellectual pursuit and theological debate. It is the experiential knowledge that transforms a person's life.

Eternal life also has a future element. The day is coming when we will be ushered into the presence of God to live forever. It is this hope that enables believers to persevere through the trials of life. The rich young man wanted to gain eternal life without a life change (Matthew 19:17–22) but discovered that the future reality is connected to present reality. Heaven isn't humanity's default destination; it is the alternate. The default destination is hell. If a person does nothing to change that destination, eternity in hell becomes the reality.[2]

Eternal life isn't just something to be obtained after death. The abundant life of John 10:10 is only possible for the one who has gained access to heaven through a saving relationship with Jesus Christ. The good life today isn't possible any other way.

This life is only temporary. Even if life continues for one hundred years, it is short in relation to eternity. Where we will spend eternity is a much bigger deal than where we spend today.

In the midst of life's problems and heartaches, never forget: This life is only temporary. One day all our burdens will be cast aside, and we will be with Christ forever.

BILLY GRAHAM
The Journey

RETHINK

When you were younger, maybe you imagined your destiny. It was full of childhood dreams of being something that might have seemed out of reach at the time. Yet childish thoughts seldom eliminate any possibilities. Today, you can have that same thought about a destiny that might seem unreal or unreachable. You can dream about heaven and know for a fact that you are going to spend eternity there.

When your life is over, what do you want to have been your most significant contribution to the world?

_____

_____

_____

_____

What are you doing right now to achieve that goal?

_____

_____

_____

_____

Most people carefully plan for their future financial security. From 401(k) plans to Roth IRAs, we are more intent than ever before to provide for our futures and the futures of our family members.

In the space below, list some of the things you are doing to prepare for your future.

_____

_____

_____

_____

As important as the future is, it is more important that we plan for eternity. What you do right now will not only affect this life, but also the life to come.

REFLECT

How can you know for certain that you have secured your eternal future through a personal relationship with Jesus Christ? Think back to the time when you first accepted Christ as your Savior and Lord. What happened then? What has happened since then? How have you seen God at work in and through your life?

Now think about your acceptance of the conditions of receiving eternal life. Here are some things that must take place in response to your faith in God.

1. **Renounce the world and its ways.**

   You can't have it both ways; you either have a relationship with Jesus Christ or you are committed to the ways of the world. But what are the ways of the world?

   Read Galatians 5:19–21 and identify any of the characteristics listed in that passage that are present in your life.

   _____

   _____

   _____

   _____

   _____

These are characteristics of a life that still is under control of self rather than God. Don't be mistaken; becoming a believer will not make these desires go away. But these worldly characteristics simply must not be the norm for someone who has real faith in Jesus Christ.

Read Luke 18:28–30. What must you renounce in order to establish faith in God?

_____

_____

_____

_____

2. **Commit your life to Christ.**

The sacrifice of Jesus Christ is a fact of faith; it is not a question. Some people add Jesus to their collection of good-luck charms they hope will gain them access to heaven. Faith in Christ is not an option.

Read John 3:16–17. What are the steps necessary to receive eternal life?

_____

_____

_____

_____

What is the difference between making a decision and making a commitment?

_____

_____

_____

_____

_____

Jesus encountered many people who made decisions to follow Him but never made a commitment. The disciples made commitments; they followed Jesus Christ and invested time learning from Him. Others made a decision to follow Christ and went away when the pressure was on.

You can go through life convinced you have made a commitment when all you have done is made a decision. Only you can determine which one you made—a decision or a commitment.

3. **Invest your life in service to God.**
   Authentic commitment to Christ results in service to God. It's not a chore; it is a privilege.

Think about your service to God. Which word best character-
izes it?

_____ A pleasure

_____ A chore

_____ A bit of both

Read John 4:35–36. When was the last time you invested time
harvesting for God?

_____

_____

_____

Service to God isn't something you plan to do in the future. The
Scripture teaches that the harvest is available right now. You know
of people who are not in right relationships with Jesus Christ. As
a follower of Christ, it is your responsibility to do the things that
are important to God. The most important act of service for any
believer is that of helping lead others to faith in Christ.

4. **Sacrifice yourself for the benefit of the kingdom.**
   Our world is fixated on entitlement. Many people
   believe they are entitled to things that earlier

generations worked to achieve. Many of the things people feel entitled to are self-centered. It's a character quality that is contrary to the working of the Holy Spirit in the lives of believers.

Read John 12:25. This verse challenges a popular way of thinking. How does the world view life, and what does this verse say in response to that belief?

_____

_____

_____

_____

_____

Christians must resist the temptation to put themselves in God's place. God demands that we maximize our commitment to Him and His purposes while minimizing our commitment to self and our own desires.

Is your life controlled by your commitment to God or to self?
Explain your response.

_____

_____

_____

_____

5. **Grow in your knowledge of God.**
   Authentic faith results in a desire to know God more.
   Knowing God is different from knowing about God.
   The knowledge of God is the result of an intimate
   relationship with the King of kings. As we know
   Him better, we take on His ways and His thoughts.

Read John 17:3. How does someone get to know God better?

_____

_____

_____

_____

To what extent are you doing these things?

_____

_____

_____

6. **Plant seeds that produce spiritual fruit.**

   We are not responsible for saving anyone; the act of salvation can only be accomplished by God. We are, however, responsible for accurately representing the gospel to the world around us. We often think about evangelistic meetings and church functions as ways to plant seeds, but there are everyday activities that can help people see who God really is.

Read Galatians 6:8. What are some things that are considered "sowing to please the sinful nature"?

_____

_____

_____

What are some things that are considered "sowing to please God"?

_____

_____

_____

_____

Are you investing more time sowing the seeds of the sinful nature or sowing seeds that please God?

_____

_____

_____

_____

REACT

There are many things that we can do to better reflect God's love to our community. I once heard a server at a restaurant lament having to work on Sunday because "the church crowd is so demanding and such poor tippers." What a tragic testimony for God's children. When we enter a place of business, people should have no doubt that we have been changed by the power of the Holy Spirit.

We are never given the privilege of being rude and demanding. We don't have the option of treating people any way other than the way God would treat them. We are not entitled to the best seat, the best service, or star treatment. We are servants of the King. We exist for His pleasure. Satan would like for us to forget that fact, and unfortunately some Christians have done just that.

Describe your relationship with God and what it means to you.

_____

_____

_____

_____

_____

Pray, asking God to make His presence stronger in your life, then live in obedience to Him. It's the good life that no one can imagine living. You and I should be humbled that God loved us enough to make us His children so that we could have this life and the life to come.

> *The Christian life is a new journey—one that will take us the rest of our lives. And we never walk it alone for Christ walks with us.*
>
> Billy Graham
> *The Journey*

What are three truths you learned in this study, and how will you apply each truth to your daily life?

1. _____

_____

_____

_____

2. _____

_____

_____

_____

_____

3. _____

_____

_____

_____

NOTES

CHAPTER 1

1. Bob Kelly, *Worth Repeating*, 2003. Grand Rapids, MI: Kregel Publications, 292.
2. *Holman Illustrated Bible Dictionary*, 2003. Nashville, TN: B&H, 799.

CHAPTER 2

1. Bob Kelly, *Worth Repeating*, 40.
2. *Holman Illustrated Bible Dictionary*, 1371–1372.

CHAPTER 3

1. Bob Kelly, *Worth Repeating*, 293.
2. *Holman Illustrated Bible Dictionary*, 47.

CHAPTER 4

1. Bob Kelly, *Worth Repeating*, 293.
2. *Holman Illustrated Bible Dictionary*, 563–565.

CHAPTER 5

1. Bob Kelly, *Worth Repeating*, 288.

CHAPTER 6

1. Bob Kelly, *Worth Repeating*, 82.
2. *Holman Illustrated Bible Dictionary*, 511–512.

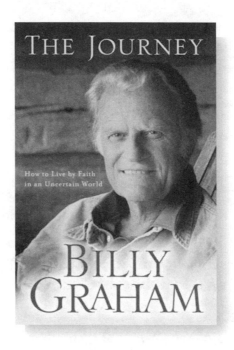

Billy Graham is respected and loved around the world.
The Journey is his magnum opus, the culmination of a
lifetime of experience and ministry. With insight that comes
only from a life spent with God, this book is filled with
wisdom, encouragement, hope, and inspiration for anyone
who wants to live a happier, more fulfilling life.

978-0-8499-1887-2 (PB)